Becoming God's Dream and the Devil's Nightmare

Henry Isaac Williams

Edited by
Nicole Queen

VISION PUBLISHING
HOUSE

Vision Publishing House
support@vision-publishinghouse.com
www.vision-publishinghouse.com

ISBN: 978-1-955297-86-8 (print)
LCCN: 2025904668

To every person carrying a dream within them…
To those who find themselves lost in the endless possibilities
of what their life could become…
To those who, at times, have felt tempted to give up…

This book is for you.

Being confident of this, that he who began a good work in you will carry it on to completion until the day of Christ Jesus.

— Philippians 1:6 (NIV)

Contents

Part Three
Prayers for Strength, Faith, & Restoration

Introduction

What began as a simple journal entry in the winter of 2015—written to encourage myself—soon transformed into a sermon, and now, this book. I never imagined that those early reflections would one day find their way into your hands. Yet, here we are. And I do not believe it is by accident.

Before you took your first breath, before you ever faced life's trials and triumphs, God had already chosen you. Every aspect of who you are—your gender, gifts, talents, strengths, and even your weaknesses—was intentionally woven into a divine master plan. You are not a mistake. You were created by God, who is love, and your existence carries immeasurable value and purpose.

Yet, life has a way of making us forget who we are. Adversity, setbacks, and disappointments can leave us questioning our significance and doubting our potential. Some of the greatest challenges we face stem from grief—the pain of loss, betrayal, and disappointment. Just as Joseph's journey led him through seasons of suffering before stepping into his predestined plan, we, too, must navigate the valleys of grief before reaching the mountaintop of purpose. Grief is not the end of the road; it is a passage that refines, strengthens, and prepares us for greater things.

This book is not only about discovering your God-given identity and dreams, but also about healing. Grief and purpose often go hand in hand, and learning to process pain in a healthy way is essential to stepping into all that God has for you. That is why prayer is woven throughout these pages—prayers of faith, hope, provision, and restoration. These prayers serve as a spiritual anchor, reminding you that no matter what you have lost, God is still writing your story.

This book is a call to awaken the extraordinary within you—to become God's Dream and the Devil's Nightmare. As you journey through these pages, may you find renewed faith, healing from past wounds, and a fresh vision for your future. May you walk confidently in your divine purpose, knowing that even through sorrow, joy will come. Your story is still unfolding, and the best is yet to come.

Part One

The Process of Becoming

Becoming all that God has called you to be is a journey that requires transformation, perseverance, and faith. *Before stepping into purpose, there is always a process.* Like Joseph, whose story is woven throughout this section, we must face tests, endure trials, and trust that even in hardship, God is shaping us for something greater.

In this section, we explore the key stages of personal growth and preparation. You will learn about the challenges of stepping into your calling, the faith required to navigate uncertainty, and the patience necessary for God's perfect timing. We will examine how dreams can lead to trials, how identity must be refined, and how obedience leads to elevation.

No matter where you are in your journey, *trust the process.* God is molding you into something far greater than you can imagine. What may seem like setbacks are actually setups, and your trials are making you stronger, wiser, and more equipped for the purpose ahead. *You are becoming.*

Chapter 1

Mr. Grape & Mr. Wine

> God often takes us through the process of crushing
> not to destroy us, but to produce something greater
> within us.
>
> — Unknown

et's take a journey to Monte Bello Vineyard in the Santa Cruz Mountains, home to some of California's finest wineries. Above your head hangs a cluster of deep purple grapes, ripe and full of potential. Within this cluster, a choice must be made.

"Mr. Grape," I say, "will you remain on the vine, comfortable and unchanged? Or will you join the others who are about to embark on the process of transformation—becoming something far greater than they are now?"

Mr. Grape ponders for a moment before asking, "What are my other options?"

"Well," I respond, "you could be sold at a local farmers' market for $6.99 a pound."

"That's it?" Mr. Grape frowns. "I believe I'm worth more than that." "Or," I continue, "you could dry out and become a raisin, waiting on a store shelf until someone tosses you into a salad or snack mix."

Mr. Grape looks even more displeased. "That doesn't sound appealing. Is there another way?"

"Yes," I say with a knowing smile. "You could become wine. The most expensive wines, like Domaine de la Romanée-Conti Grand Cru, are sought after by the wealthiest people in the world. You could be served in royal ballrooms, poured into fine crystal glasses, and savored for your rich complexity and depth."

Mr. Grape's eyes widen with excitement. "That sounds incredible! What must I do to be honored and valued like that?"

"Well," I say, "to reach that level, you must first endure the process. You won't look the same as you do now. You will be crushed, pressed underfoot until every drop of your essence is extracted. Then, you'll be purified, stored, and aged for years—perhaps even decades—before you are ready to be poured into greatness." Mr. Grape hesitates. "That sounds painful."

"Yes," I nod. "But are you willing to go through it? Are you ready to surrender who you are now to become who you were destined to be?"

And now, dear reader, I ask you the same question. This book is for those who are willing to endure the process of transformation—those who are ready to become God's dream and the devil's nightmare.

* * *

Heavenly Father, I surrender myself to Your process, even when it feels uncomfortable. Just as grapes must be crushed to become fine wine, I trust that the challenges I face are shaping me into who You've called me to be. Give me the patience to endure, the wisdom to grow, and the faith to believe that what You are producing in me is far greater than anything I could imagine. May my life be a testament to Your transforming power.

In Jesus' Name, Amen.

Chapter 2

What's Age Got to Do With It?

> Even in old age they will still produce fruit; they will remain vital and green.
>
> — Psalm 92:14 (NLT)

Let's consider Abram at 75 years old—a stage in life when many people are settling into comfort, avoiding risks, and focusing on securing their legacy through wills, estates, and retirement plans. Yet, in the midst of what most would consider the winding-down years, God called Abram into something entirely new.

In Genesis 12, we see that Abram was commanded to leave his father's house and journey to a land he had never seen, where he would become the founder of a great nation. Obediently, he departed with his wife, Sarai, and his nephew, Lot, whom he had adopted after his brother's passing.

Despite his faith, Abram carried many limited mindsets and perspectives, shaped by his past and circumstances. His journey truly began when he first received the prophecy, yet it was his willingness to act on God's promise that earned him the title of *the father of faith*—a designation recognized by Jewish, Islamic, and Christian communities alike.

At one point, he even gave up hope of having a son, resigning himself to the idea that his best servant would inherit his legacy. But just because we give up on a dream does not mean God does. I have met many elders who, having lived long lives, become set in their beliefs, convinced that change is no longer possible. Yet, God's faithfulness is not hindered by age.

Abram's faith was tested and refined through sacrifice. Each time God spoke to him, Abram built an altar and made an offering—a symbolic act of surrendering the old self. But his transformation didn't stop there. God gave him a new name—Abraham—signifying his shift from simply being a man, to a father, to the *father of many nations*. His wife, once barren, was renamed Sarah, the mother of kings and nations.

The process of becoming who God has called you to be will require sacrifice. For Abraham, it even included circumcision—a painful but necessary mark of covenant and commitment. Growth, transformation, and fulfillment of divine purpose always come at a cost. But in the end, what is not needed will be removed, and you will be realigned for something greater.

Abraham's story teaches us that God's plans often require us to step outside our comfort zones, even when we feel past our prime. But His promises remain true, and His timing is always perfect.

* * *

Heavenly Father, thank You for reminding me that age is never a limitation in Your kingdom. Whether young or old, You have a purpose and a plan for my life. Help me to embrace every season with faith and confidence, knowing that You can use me at any stage. Give me the courage to step into new opportunities, the wisdom to walk in Your timing, and the perseverance to keep moving forward. Let my life be a testimony that You are never done working in and through me.

In Jesus' Name, Amen.

Chapter 3

Late Bloomers Still Bloom

 There is a time for everything, and a season for every activity under the heavens.

— Ecclesiastes 3:1 (NIV)

I once read about an extraordinary event in the deserts of California. A region that had been dry for over a thousand years suddenly experienced rainfall, and to the astonishment of scientists and onlookers, miles of once-barren land erupted into a sea of vibrant flowers. It was later discovered that seeds had been carried by the wind and buried in the desert soil, lying dormant until the rain came and awakened them to bloom.

I don't know where the winds of life have carried you or how long you've been waiting, but you can still bloom. There's a saying: *bloom where you are planted.* Perhaps you feel like a rose growing through the cracks in concrete, struggling against impossible odds. But hear this—your forecast is changing, and heaven is releasing the rain you need to blossom.

God has not forgotten the buds in your life—the dreams, desires, and opportunities that have yet to unfold. I remember a minister once sharing a word of knowledge with me, saying that some opportunities I thought were lost were actually coming back around. God was opening doors I had assumed were permanently closed. That revelation reignited my joy. As I began to verbalize the dreams I had buried—the visions I had suppressed while other parts of my life flourished— I realized that God wasn't just interested in what had already bloomed; He was still invested in the buds waiting to unfold. "Though your beginning was small, your latter days will be very great." (Job 8:7)

As long as you have breath, it is not too late. I am so relieved to no longer live under the pressure of self-imposed timelines—the idea that I must accomplish certain milestones between ages 30 and 40, whether it be success in business, starting a family, or fulfilling personal goals. I am grateful for the wisdom of an apostolic psalmist from Fairbanks, Alaska, who once told me, "Henry, break the stopwatch of your life. Your times and seasons are in God's hands."

That gentle reproof from Apostle Cross freed me from unnecessary stress. We often place heavy burdens on ourselves, rushing to make our God-given dreams a reality, only to create a nightmare through impatience and poor judgment. In our haste, we can settle for *good* instead of waiting for *God's best*.

God has used many—including myself—to challenge and stretch others in their faith. It's not always easy; in fact, it can be frustrating and difficult. But love compels us to keep pushing forward. Why? Because so many are on the brink of their promise, standing at the edge of their predestined plan, needing only one last Holy Ghost push to cross over.

You were born an individual, but you will leave this world a nation. You may have entered life in poverty, but you will leave it rich. You were born as one, but you will depart as an institution, an author, an educator, a legend.

It doesn't matter how you start—it's how you finish that counts. Abraham had to change his mindset from believing he was too old and unqualified to have a child, to embracing God's promise. Becoming God's dream requires a renewed vocabulary. Words like "can't" and "never" must be evicted from your heart so that you speak only in agreement with the plan God has designed for you.

Let the weak say, "I am strong." Let the poor say, "I am rich."

Your season of blooming is here.

* * *

Heavenly Father, thank You for reminding me that timing is in Your hands. Just as You bring forth flowers in their due season, I trust that my purpose and calling will unfold according to Your perfect plan. Help me not to compare my journey to others, but to walk confidently in the path You have set before me. Give me patience in the waiting, strength in the process, and faith to believe that I will bloom in due time. Let my life be a testament to Your faithfulness.

In Jesus' Name, Amen.

Chapter 4

Wow, That Hurt!

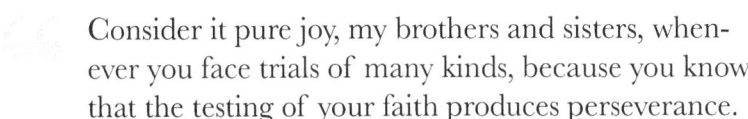

Consider it pure joy, my brothers and sisters, whenever you face trials of many kinds, because you know that the testing of your faith produces perseverance.

—James 1:2-3 (NIV)

I know, Mr. Grape, that since you have chosen to become honorable wine, you are now experiencing the pressing and crushing. This process is not easy—it is uncomfortable, even painful. But it is necessary.

If you have studied the lives of Abraham and Sarah, you may have noticed how their flaws were exposed along the journey to their promise. Abraham lied, Sarah doubted, and both grew impatient. Manipulation and infidelity unfolded as they attempted to bring God's vision to pass in their own way.

Likewise, God allows trials to expose what is within us—not to shame us, but to remove what is unnecessary. Just as the skins of the grape must be stripped away so that only the pure juice remains, God is refining you, separating what must stay from what must go. Anything that could hinder your future will rise to the surface, but do not be discouraged. God knew exactly who you were before He called and chose you. He loves you far more than the hindrances He is working to remove.

As a teacher at heart, I have often encountered resistance when confronting mindsets that do not serve God's purpose. Some have mistaken my words as personal attacks, but my battle has never been with individuals—it has always been against toxic thinking. Transformation requires challenge, and true growth demands a willingness to let go of old, limiting beliefs. The process may feel like crushing, but it is producing something far greater within you.

* * *

Heavenly Father, pain is a reality of life, but I trust that You never waste my hurt. You see every tear, every heartbreak, and every disappointment. When the wounds feel deep, remind me that You are deeper still. Strengthen my heart to endure, and give me wisdom to grow through my struggles rather than be defined by them. Let Your love heal the broken places within me, and may I emerge from this season stronger, wiser, and more like You.

In Jesus' Name, Amen.

Chapter 5

Looking for God's Plan

 Many are the plans in a person's heart, but it is the
Lord's purpose that prevails.

— Proverbs 19:21 (NIV)

The original rough draft of this book sat untouched in my
closet for six years. I had forgotten where I placed it, and
when I felt led by faith to write a revised version, I initially
believed the original was already perfect. But when I finally found it
and began reading, I realized something profound—losing it was a
blessing. By the time I was halfway through, I knew this version was
better.

A revised version is always better than the original. We often
expect life to unfold in a specific way, with certain people or circumstances aligning perfectly. But God's thoughts are higher, and His
ways are beyond our comprehension. Abraham assumed Lot would
journey with him forever. He believed his servant would be his heir,
that Hagar would always be Sarah's maid, and that Ishmael would
inherit the messianic promise. But God had a different plan.

The most successful people learn to treat failures as stepping stones, using them as lessons that refine them rather than define them. Sacrifice is costly, but it is also necessary. When God tested Abraham, it wasn't to take something away from him, but to see if Abraham would withhold anything from the Lord.

We can become so zealous and eager to see our vision come to life, but what if what we see is only a piece of something much greater? Right now, you may be focused on launching your dream as a solo endeavor, but what if God designed it to be a partnership? What if you are meant to be the visionary but not the builder? What if you need a team?

Sometimes, we must let go of the idea of being the lone hero so we can step into something bigger—like a "Justice League" style of business, where every gift, talent, and strength has a purpose, just as every part of the body plays a vital role. Two are always better than one; when one falls, the other can lift them up.

I remember developing two curricula and being fully prepared to execute one myself. But the Lord told me to entrust it to someone else, making them the face of it. Initially, this challenged my thinking, but when I obeyed, it became far more successful than I could have imagined. I had to understand my place in the master plan, and in doing so, I saw the power of God's greater vision.

* * *

Heavenly Father, I surrender my plans, my dreams, and my uncertainties to You. Your ways are higher than mine, and Your thoughts are beyond my understanding. Help me to trust in Your timing and to seek Your wisdom in every decision. When the path ahead seems unclear, remind me that You are guiding my steps. Give me the patience to wait, the faith to believe, and the courage to follow wherever You lead. May Your purpose be fulfilled in my life.

In Jesus' Name, Amen.

Chapter 6

The Discipline of Dreamers

 Dreams don't work unless you do.

— John C. Maxwell

Studies show that fifty percent of self-made millionaires wake up at least three hours before their work schedule. Their success is not just about talent—it's about discipline, time management, and commitment to their vision.

There are two kinds of people: dreamers who buy and doers who create. Dreamers support businesses by purchasing products they *could* make themselves—if they had the time, drive, or inclination. The difference between someone like Martha Stewart, who built a $400 million empire, and those who simply use her products comes down to how they invest their time.

Time is a resource we all have in equal measure—24 hours a day. The question is: how are we using it? Are we consuming more than we create? Are we investing in our skills, businesses, and passions? Or are we making others wealthy while neglecting our own potential?

This realization led me to an unusual question: Do ants sleep? I discovered that they do, but in a way that maximizes productivity. Ants take over 150 micro-naps a day, each lasting less than a minute, ensuring they never stop working for long. The Bible says in Proverbs 6:6, "Go to the ant, you sluggard; consider her ways and be wise." These diligent workers gather food not just for their daily needs but for future seasons, preparing for winter while it is still summer.

The same principle applies to us. Success doesn't happen overnight—it is the result of small, consistent actions, just like the ant's tireless labor. When I reflect on the past ten years of social media, I realize that the time I spent scrolling and liking posts was enriching someone else's dream. But now, I choose to work on my craft, my purpose, and my calling.

God delights in our personal prosperity (Psalm 35:27), but it requires diligence. Like the ant, we must believe that the work we do today will sustain us tomorrow. Let us pray:

Lord, teach us to number our days, so that we may apply wisdom (Psalm 90:12).

*   *   *

Heavenly Father, thank You or the dreams You have placed within me. Grant me the discipline to remain steadfast in the process, even when the journey is long and challenging. Help me to stay focused, diligent, and faithful in my calling. When distractions arise, give me the strength to press forward with integrity and perseverance. Let my efforts align with Your will, and may my work bring glory to Your name.

In Jesus' Name, Amen.

Chapter 7

Believe in Yourself

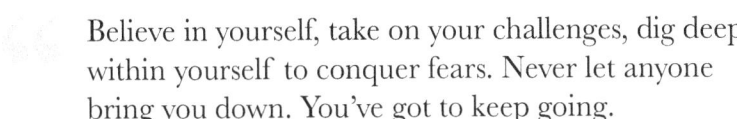 Believe in yourself, take on your challenges, dig deep within yourself to conquer fears. Never let anyone bring you down. You've got to keep going.

— Chantal Sutherland

If any Christian tells you they don't believe in themselves, they may not fully understand their identity in Christ!

Jesus never doubted who He was—He walked in complete confidence, knowing what His Father had spoken about Him. Throughout His ministry, He boldly declared:

- I am the bread of life.
- I am the true vine.
- I am the light of the world.
- I am the way, the truth, and the life.
- I am the door.
- I am the good shepherd.

Jesus never operated in inferiority, and His followers carried that same assurance, even in the face of persecution and death. They stood firm because they believed in His promise of eternal life and the rewards of faith.

But what about us? Who told you that you are weak? Who told you that you are not enough? In Genesis 3, after Adam and Eve sinned, God asked Adam, "Who told you that you were naked?" Likewise, who planted seeds of doubt in your mind?

Inferiority can paralyze us at the edge of our Promised Land—able to see the blessings ahead but too afraid to step into them. The Israelites felt like grasshoppers compared to the Canaanites, and because of their doubt, they never entered the land God had prepared for them. Joshua, however, had a different spirit—he declared, "We are well able to overcome!" Yet, the people had already been convinced by the negative report.

Overoming Feelings of Inferiority

If you ever struggle with doubt, here are three keys to overcoming it:

1. *Check the source of your inferiority mindset.* Who told you that you couldn't do it? Identify the voices that have shaped your beliefs.
2. *Discover your strengths.* God has gifted you with unique talents and abilities—recognize them.
3. *Take action.* You only have one life to live—don't let fear stop you from pursuing what God has placed inside you.

One missed opportunity is more costly than any failure. Adam's feelings of inferiority caused him to hide from God, but running away never leads to restoration. The enemy plants false narratives in our minds to keep us from stepping into our God-given purpose. Becoming God's dream and the devil's nightmare requires surrendering to His plan and trusting His vision for your life.

Confidence Comes From Sacrifice

"Great achievements are usually born from great sacrifice and are never the result of selfishness."

— Napoleon Hill

Wiley C. Harrison grew up in Queens, New York, and graduated from a tough high school in the early '70s. He worked a variety of minimum-wage jobs—digging ditches for construction, handling clerical tasks on Wall Street—until one day, he noticed something small but significant.

The knots on his colleagues' ties were sleek and smooth, while his were bulky. Upon asking, he learned their ties were $100 silk, while his were polyester. That moment sparked a realization: he wanted more for his life.

Harrison became the first in his family to attend college. He enrolled at Wilberforce University in Ohio at 23, determined to change his future. After graduating magna cum laude with a degree in accounting, he went on to earn an MBA from Columbia Business School.

After five years in corporate America, he felt unfulfilled. He no longer wanted to be just a cog in the machine—he wanted to create something meaningful. So, in 1992, he founded *Business of Your Business*, an outsourced accounting firm for nonprofit and religious organizations.

The company started small—he did personal tax returns at McDonald's or in clients' homes. But today, it employs over 10 full-time and three part-time staff, serving 750 individuals and 75 small businesses, with annual revenue of $500,000. Harrison credits his success to his empathy and personal experience:

People trust me because I've been there. I've dug ditches and I've sat in boardrooms. I've lived in the projects and owned a home in the suburbs. Right now, I feel like I am living a dream.

You are capable of more than you think. You were not created to shrink back in fear but to rise in confidence. Every great leader—whether in faith, business, or history—had moments of doubt, but they refused to let it stop them.

 Patience, persistence, and perspiration make an unbeatable combination for success.

— Estell

Like Harrison, Joshua, and Jesus the Christ Himself— believe in who God has called you to be.

* * *

Heavenly Father, thank You for creating me with purpose and strength. Help me to see myself through Your eyes and walk in the confidence of my identity in Christ. I reject fear and doubt and embrace the calling You have placed on my life. Strengthen my faith to step boldly into Your promises.

In Jesus' Name, Amen.

Chapter 8

A New Posture

 And we know that in all things God works for the good of those who love him, who have been called according to his purpose.

> — Romans 8:28 (NIV)

When a baby takes their first steps and stumbles, we cheer them on, celebrating their effort. But as we grow older, society often offers less encouragement. Instead of lifting us up, it mocks our mistakes, criticizes our missteps, and highlights what we should have done differently.

But let me remind you—don't lower your head too much; it will deform your posture. The same applies to your spirit. Don't lower yourself to pick up the trash of negative opinions about your failures.

I once went through therapy where weight was placed on my neck to correct my posture. I had to endure 15 minutes of discomfort, but the message was clear—keep your gaze lifted. The weight wasn't there to harm me but to train me to look up.

Look Up, Child

Just as Abraham was commanded to look up and see the stars as a symbol of God's promise, I challenge you to lift your eyes beyond your current circumstances. There is so much more ahead of you than what you can see right now.

Scientists estimate that there are at least 20 million stars in our solar system alone, and some stars are more than 1,500 times the size of our Sun. From the ground, they might appear as tiny flickers of light, but in reality, they are enormous celestial giants.

God's thoughts and intentions for us are just as vast—more numerous than the grains of sand. (Psalm 139:17-18) They stretch far beyond what we can comprehend. If we understood the fullness of His plan, it would expand our capacity for faith, hope, and purpose.

So today, adjust your posture. Lift your head. Fix your gaze on the God who calls you higher. You were never meant to live small— you were made to shine.

* * *

Heavenly Father, thank You for reminding me to lift my head and trust in Your greater plan. Help me to stand tall in faith, rejecting fear and discouragement. Strengthen my spirit to see beyond my present circumstances and embrace the future You have prepared for me.

In Jesus' Name, Amen.

Chapter 9

A Life Set Apart for Destiny

 Before I formed you in the womb I knew you, before
you were born I set you apart; I appointed you as a
prophet to the nations.

— Jeremiah 1:5 (NIV)

I n ancient Hebrew culture, the birth of sons was seen as a
guarantee of a family's survival and prosperity. The firstborn
son was entitled to a double portion of the inheritance—not
simply for personal gain, but as a responsibility to support aging
parents and secure the family's future. Joseph, though not the firstborn, was given a dream that set him apart. His life would not
follow the traditional path of a shepherd like his father. Instead, his
purpose would lead him from servanthood to leadership, ultimately
overseeing a nation.

His prophetic vision came through a dream—one where he saw
himself towering over the stars, with the sun and moon bowing
before him. Many believe this represented his father, Pharaoh, and
his twelve brothers, despite the fact that his mother had passed away.
However, instead of celebrating this vision, his brothers felt threat-

ened. It is often the case that people struggle to see you outside of the box they have placed you in. When they hear your dreams, they may become offended, not because of your ambition, but because your vision challenges their limited mindset.

Joseph was given a coat of many colors, a sign of his father's special favor. But favor comes with responsibility—and sometimes, rejection. If you have ever felt different, out of place, or misunderstood, you are in good company. Like Joseph, you may be set apart for something greater. God does not call us according to human traditions but according to His divine purpose.

The Excitement and the Cost of a Dream

The passion of having a God-given dream is exhilarating. We can become so focused on our own aspirations that we forget the One who gave them to us. Many world changers—those who founded charities, created medical breakthroughs, or pioneered great movements—were driven by their own painful experiences. Sometimes, our personal struggles prepare us for a greater calling.

Joseph was excited about his dream and shared it with his brothers, expecting their support. Instead, he was met with resentment. Not everyone will celebrate your vision. Rejection from those closest to you can be painful, but it can also be purposeful. If Joseph had not been betrayed, he would not have reached his predestined plan. The Bible reminds us:

> Enlarge the place of your tent, stretch your tent curtains wide, do not hold back; lengthen your cords, strengthen your stakes.
>
> — Isaiah 54:2

If we are to step into the fullness of our calling, we must expand our capacity for growth, relationships, and faith. If we do not, we risk becoming dream killers—those who discourage others because of our own limitations.

Betrayed, Rejected, and Left for Dead

Joseph's own brothers plotted against him. As they watched over their flocks, they saw him approaching from a distance. They conspired to kill him, strip him of his coat, and cast him into a pit. Instead, Judah intervened and convinced them to sell him into slavery.

The pit represents a place of helplessness, where we feel trapped and unable to escape. Joseph found himself at the mercy of others, just as many of us find ourselves overwhelmed by situations beyond our control—financial struggles, betrayals, broken relationships, or personal failures. But what seemed like an ending was really a divine setup.

Joseph was sold into slavery and taken to Egypt. His brothers thought they had removed him from their lives, but in doing so, they unknowingly set him on the path to his predestined place. Even the most painful betrayals can be used for God's greater purpose.

Genesis recounts how Joseph's brothers deceived their father, Jacob:

> They took Joseph's robe, slaughtered a goat, and dipped the robe in the blood… Their father recognized it and said, 'It is my son's robe! A wild animal must have devoured him. Joseph has surely been torn to pieces.'
>
> — Genesis 37:31-36

Jacob mourned deeply, refusing to be comforted, believing his beloved son was lost forever. But what man thought was the end, God was only beginning.

From the Pit to Purpose

Joseph's journey was one of betrayal, suffering, and ultimately, redemption. His trials were not for nothing—they were preparing him for a place of influence and leadership. The very people who rejected him would one day stand before him in need.

If you feel like you are in the pit—forgotten, overlooked, or struggling—know that God has not abandoned you. Your story is not over. What others meant for evil, God will use for good. (Genesis 50:20)

* * *

Heavenly Father, for those who feel abandoned, betrayed, or trapped in a pit, remind them that You are in control. You see their pain, and You are working all things together for their good. Strengthen their hearts, renew their faith, and give them the courage to trust Your process. What others meant for harm, You will turn into purpose.

In Jesus' Name, Amen.

Chapter 10

Faithfulness in the Unknown

Trust in the Lord with all your heart, and do not lean on your own understanding. In all your ways acknowledge him, and he will make straight your paths.

— Proverbs 3:5-6 (ESV)

Every dreamer knows the sting of rejection and the challenge of adapting to unfamiliar surroundings. Joseph, once favored in his father's house, found himself in Egypt, a foreign land with a new culture, language, and way of life. Stripped of his past identity, he was given an Egyptian name and placed in Potiphar's house as a servant. Yet, this was not the end of his story—*it was the beginning of his preparation.*

Before anyone can lead, they must first serve. Joseph's time in Potiphar's house was an entry-level course in leadership—he had to understand the responsibilities of management, the discipline of stewardship, and the importance of integrity. Scripture tells us that "the Lord was with Joseph" (Genesis 39:2), and as a result, everything he touched prospered. Potiphar recognized this favor and entrusted Joseph with overseeing his entire household.

This is what I call *The Trust Factor*—the principle that before God entrusts you with your own vision, He will first test you with someone else's. Can you serve another's dream with faithfulness? Can you be counted on when no one is watching? Being reliable and working with integrity is more valuable than money because it is the currency of promotion in God's kingdom.

The Test of Temptation

Temptation is not something we can avoid, but it is something we can prepare for. Joseph faced one of the most dangerous tests of all —the temptation to compromise his integrity for temporary gain. Potiphar's wife pursued him relentlessly, offering him what seemed like an easy opportunity to indulge in sin without consequence.

Joseph had a choice: Give in and satisfy the moment or flee and safeguard his future. He understood a powerful truth: "How then can I do this great wickedness and sin against God?" (Genesis 39:9).

Integrity is not a burden; it is a standard of living. Saying "yes" to compromise often means saying "no" to God's best. Many dreamers on their way to success have been trapped by moral failure because they didn't flee when they had the chance.

What happens in secret never remains hidden forever. Many leaders who fell into scandal did not fail in public—they first failed in private. Joseph's story teaches us that we must not entertain what we should be running from. Temptation will come, but like Joseph, we must be prepared to flee before it overtakes us.

From Paradise to Purpose

God created the world in perfection, but through Adam and Eve's disobedience, sin entered and brought with it sickness, deception, and loss. Though we live in a broken world, we can find comfort in knowing that God is a master at transforming what was meant for evil into good (Romans 8:28).

Joseph's life was not just a story of success; it was a story of breaking generational cycles. His family history was marked by jealousy, rivalry, and division—from Isaac and Ishmael to Jacob and Esau—and now, the pattern had reached him and his brothers. But Joseph's pain was not wasted—God used it to set a new course for his family's future.

Many of the struggles we face today did not start with us, but they can end with us. The rejection Joseph experienced was necessary to position him for his purpose. The very thing meant to destroy him became the catalyst for his elevation.

Your Gifts Will Make Room for You

Joseph's ability to interpret dreams opened the door to his purpose. He had always been gifted, but in the right environment, his gift was recognized and valued. When Pharaoh had troubling dreams, it was Joseph's wisdom that brought clarity—and it was this wisdom that made him second-in-command over all of Egypt.

Your gifts are not random—they are the keys to your destiny. What comes naturally to you? What do you enjoy doing, even without payment? The answers to these questions often point to the purpose God has placed inside of you.

A mentor once asked me, "What would you do every day, even if no one paid you for it?" That question changed my perspective. Joseph didn't just have a gift; he used his gift—even in a prison cell. Your gift is the currency that will position you before great people. But before that happens, you must be willing to refine it, develop it, and use it even when no one is watching.

Reclaiming Dominion

Adam and Eve lost dominion, but through Christ, we regain it. Likewise, Joseph lost everything—his home, his family, his freedom —yet God restored him to a position greater than what he had before.

Joseph's story is a reminder that our trials are never wasted. If you feel forgotten, overlooked, or stuck in an unexpected place, know this: God is working behind the scenes. Just because you don't see movement doesn't mean progress isn't happening.

Like Joseph, you are being prepared, refined, and positioned for something greater. Your journey is not a detour—it is divine preparation. Hold on. *Stay faithful.* The best is yet to come.

* * *

Heavenly Father, thank You for being my anchor in seasons of uncertainty. When I can't see the way forward, help me trust that You are leading me. Strengthen my heart to remain faithful even when the outcome is unclear. Let my obedience in the unknown prepare me for the fulfillment of Your promises. I surrender my plans to You and choose to walk in faith.

In Jesus' Name, Amen.

Chapter 11

From the Dungeon to the Palace

Do you see a man skillful in his work? He will stand
before kings; he will not stand before obscure men.

— Proverbs 22:29 (ESV)

For three years, Joseph faithfully used his gifts to serve others
in prison. He interpreted dreams, offered wisdom, and
remained steadfast, yet he might have felt forgotten and
undervalued. It seemed as though no one recognized his efforts, but
God was preparing him for something greater.

Faithfulness in small things is a test of character. If we remain
diligent with what we have now, God will entrust us with more.
Joseph's prison experience wasn't a dead end; it was divine preparation. Then, one day, everything changed—Pharaoh had a problem,
and Joseph had the solution.

Imagine the moment when Joseph was summoned before the
most powerful man in Egypt. He went from being a forgotten prisoner to standing before a king. This was a life-altering opportunity,

yet it came suddenly. Have you ever considered how you would react if someone influential called on you?

Many people hesitate when presented with a major opportunity. Doubt, fear, and feelings of inadequacy can creep in. I remember moments when I was sought after by prominent figures, yet I wrestled with uncertainty—Am I ready? What if I fail? But I've learned that opportunities don't always wait for us to feel ready. If we hesitate too long, we risk missing our moment.

Preparing for the Opportunity

Egyptians were known for their meticulous attention to appearance and hygiene. In a culture where presentation mattered, Joseph's prison clothes were unsuitable for a royal audience. Yet, God provided everything he needed to be ready.

In just one day, Joseph underwent a transformation. He was washed, groomed, and dressed appropriately before stepping into his predestined place. This was not just about looking presentable—it symbolized how God prepares us for divine appointments.

Sometimes, before we walk into our calling, God will refine us, reposition us, and remove anything that could hinder us. He will provide the right people, resources, and circumstances to ensure we are equipped for what's ahead. Don't resist the process of preparation—God is working behind the scenes.

Standing Before Pharaoh

Genesis 41 tells us that Joseph, once bound in chains, now stood before Pharaoh. Yet, even in this defining moment, Joseph remained humble. He didn't boast about his ability to interpret dreams. Instead, he declared, "I cannot do it, but God will give Pharaoh the answer he desires" (Genesis 41:16).

Joseph's story reminds us that favor comes in appointed seasons. If Joseph had received favor too soon, he might have focused on finding his family rather than fulfilling his greater purpose. God's timing was perfect. The very skills Joseph developed in obscurity were now the key to his elevation.

His time in prison was not wasted. It taught him discipline, patience, and stewardship. When the moment came, he didn't let past disappointments hold him back. He was ready to step into his purpose.

Embrace Your Preparation

Joseph's journey is a testament to God's faithfulness. Even in difficult and painful seasons, God is preparing us for something greater.

If you feel like you're in a waiting season, don't lose heart. What looks like a delay is often preparation. Be faithful in the small things, and trust that when the time is right, God will position you for greater things.

* * *

Heavenly Father, thank You for the seasons of preparation. When I feel forgotten, remind me that You are working behind the scenes. Help me to remain faithful in the small things, knowing that nothing is wasted in Your hands. Refine me, equip me, and position me for the opportunities You have prepared for me. May I walk in confidence, knowing that Your timing is perfect.

In Jesus' Name, Amen.

Chapter 12

Becoming the Solution

The Lord will make you the head and not the tail; you shall be above only, and not beneath, if you heed the commandments of the Lord your God and are careful to observe them.

— Deuteronomy 28:13 (NKJV)

Living out God's dream for our lives means stepping into responsibility, embracing challenges, and providing solutions where others have not. Instead of waiting for someone else to take action, God is calling you to rise up and be the answer.

Joseph exemplified this truth when he identified Pharaoh's problem and devised a strategic plan to save millions from famine. His wisdom, insight, and faithfulness turned a national crisis into an opportunity for divine intervention. What if the solution to someone's challenge lies within you?

Many are willing to invest significant resources in finding answers. What unique skills, ideas, or innovations has God placed inside of you? You may be the Joseph or Josephine of your field—uniquely positioned to provide what others cannot.

Rising to Leadership

Leadership is not about a title or position—it's about vision, passion, purpose, and responsibility. Joseph's rise from prison to power reminds us that God often promotes those who remain faithful in the unseen places. His journey teaches us that leadership emerges from the most unexpected places, even from the trials and setbacks we endure.

Imagine the shift Joseph experienced—from being a forgotten prisoner to standing before Pharaoh, the most powerful ruler of his time. In a single day, he was transformed from a servant into a leader, entrusted with the governance of an entire nation.

Joseph's story reminds us that God's plans will always elevate us beyond our limitations. Even when life seems unfair, even when doors appear closed, God is working behind the scenes, preparing you for a greater assignment.

Step Into Your Purpose

Have you ever doubted whether you are truly meant to lead? You don't need to have everything figured out—God qualifies the called. He sees beyond your fears, weaknesses, and limitations. Just as Pharaoh recognized Joseph's potential, God is positioning you for your divine assignment.

Your talents, experiences, and trials have not been wasted. Every challenge has prepared you for this moment. Will you embrace the call to be a solution? Will you step forward into the purpose God has been shaping within you?

* * *

Heavenly Father, thank You for the gifts and abilities You have placed within me. I surrender my fears, doubts, and limitations to You. Help me recognize the divine opportunities You set before me. Give me wisdom, boldness, and humility as I step into my purpose. May I be a solution to the problems around me and use my influence to glorify You.

In Jesus' Name, Amen.

Chapter 13

The Unavoidable Crossroad

Weeping may endure for a night, but joy comes in the morning.

— Psalm 30:5 (KJV)

As we reflect on Joseph's journey, we see how his faithfulness and perseverance ultimately led him into abundance. Yet, his story was not without deep sorrow, loss, and betrayal. Before stepping into his purpose, Joseph endured seasons of rejection, separation, and suffering. His life reminds us that grief and purpose often go hand in hand.

We've explored what it means to fulfill God's dream— overcoming challenges and stepping into divine purpose. But one reality we cannot ignore is grief—a common thread throughout human experience. Just as Joseph learned to navigate his pain, we, too, must learn how to process, heal, and grow from our own experiences of loss.

In the next section, we will explore:

- Joseph's strategic plan during the seven years of plenty and famine
- How Joseph's trials positioned him to bless his family and an entire nation
- How grief, when surrendered to God, can shape us into the people He has called us to be

Understanding Grief as Part of Life's Journey

Joseph was born into privilege and promise, growing up in a wealthy family destined for greatness. His very existence was a miracle, the fulfillment of a promise made to his parents in their old age. From the beginning, he was set apart, and the blessings spoken over his bloodline positioned him for an extraordinary calling.

Yet, great callings often come with great challenges. To fully step into his divine destiny, Joseph had to endure betrayal, isolation, and deep grief. Without spiritual maturity, emotional resilience, and divine wisdom, he might have been crushed under the weight of his trials.

Grief is an unavoidable part of the human experience. It was never part of God's original plan, but in a fallen world, it has become something we must all confront. Grief disrupts our sense of normalcy, shakes our faith, and forces us to confront loss in all its forms—the loss of relationships, dreams, expectations, or even our sense of identity. However, grief also has the power to refine us, shaping us into stronger, wiser, and more compassionate individuals.

Even Scripture acknowledges the depth of Joseph's suffering:

> They bruised his feet with shackles; his neck was put in irons. He sent a man before them—Joseph, sold as a slave. Until the time his word came to pass, the word of the Lord tested him.
>
> — Psalm 105:18

Joseph's trials were not a sign of abandonment but a preparation for promotion. The tests that God allows in our lives are not meant to break us but to expand our capacity—preparing us to steward the callings, responsibilities, and positions of influence He has planned for us.

If you find yourself walking through a season of grief, take heart. God is still at work, shaping your pain into purpose, refining your character, and preparing you for the future He has ordained for you.

* * *

Heavenly Father, I come before You with a heart that has known sorrow and loss. Thank You for reminding me that You are close to the brokenhearted and that You turn mourning into joy. Help me trust that my pain is not wasted but is shaping me for greater purpose. Teach me to lean on You in moments of grief, and give me the strength to embrace the healing and restoration You have promised. May I walk forward in faith, knowing that You are working all things together for my good.

In Jesus' Name, Amen.

Part Two

Navigating Grief

Grief is an inevitable part of the human experience, yet it is often misunderstood or avoided. It comes in many forms—loss of a loved one, the end of a relationship, missed opportunities, or even the death of a dream. While grief can feel overwhelming, it is not meant to leave us broken; rather, it is a process that God can use to *refine*, *restore*, and *reposition* us for greater purpose.

In this section, we will explore how to navigate grief through faith, embrace healing, and allow God to transform our pain into purpose. Using biblical examples—particularly the life of Joseph—we will see that grief does not have to define us, but can instead shape us into stronger, more compassionate, and more purpose-driven individuals.

Healing is a journey, not a destination. As you walk through this section, may you find comfort in knowing that you are not alone. God is with you, holding every tear and guiding you toward restoration.

Chapter 14

The Journey Through Loss and Separation

 The Lord is close to the brokenhearted and saves those who are crushed in spirit.

— Psalm 34:18 (NIV)

Throughout history, and even in some cultures today, being present with a loved one in their final moments is a deeply cherished custom—a chance to say goodbye, to hold their hand, and to find closure. But Joseph never had this opportunity. His mother, Rachel, died while giving birth to his younger brother, Benjamin. Before he could fully grieve her loss, his life took an unexpected turn. Betrayed by his brothers and sold into slavery, Joseph was forced into a future he never asked for, carrying the weight of loss without the comfort of family to help him process it.

Can you imagine the depth of sorrow he must have felt? The pain of never hearing his mother's voice again, of never receiving her embrace, of never saying goodbye? Some wounds linger not because we want them to, but because life never gave us the chance to close them properly.

What do we do with grief that remains unresolved? How do we

heal when closure seems impossible? These are the questions we must confront as we navigate loss. The good news is that even when we feel abandoned in our grief, God is near. His presence brings the healing our hearts long for, even when circumstances don't provide the closure we seek.

* * *

Heavenly Father, You see the wounds in our hearts—the losses we never got to process, the goodbyes we never got to say. Remind us that even when closure seems impossible, Your love is our refuge. Heal the broken places within us and bring peace where there is pain. Help us to trust that You are near, even in the midst of sorrow.

In Jesus' Name, Amen.

Chapter 15

Facing the Past and Letting Go

Forget the former things; do not dwell on the past.
See, I am doing a new thing! Now it springs up; do
you not perceive it?

— Isaiah 43:18-19 (NIV)

Joseph's leadership during the famine brought him international recognition, elevating him to a position of power and influence. But when he unexpectedly encountered his brothers—the very ones who had betrayed him—long-buried wounds resurfaced. His story is a reminder that even as our dreams unfold and we step into new seasons of success, unresolved pain from the past can reappear.

God, the master gardener of our lives, knows when to prune and when to cultivate. He allows past hurts to surface—not to break us, but to heal us. The fears, disappointments, and painful memories that arise as we move forward are not setbacks; they are opportunities for refinement and restoration.

Facing the Past

Joseph's response to seeing his brothers teaches us an important truth: while pain and trauma are real, they do not have to define our future. I remember a time when I unexpectedly came face-to-face with someone who had deeply wounded me. A flood of emotions rushed in, but instead of being consumed by anger, I saw an opportunity for growth and healing.

Healing from past wounds is essential. Whether through counseling, journaling, prayer, or other means, processing pain allows us to transform past sorrows into strength. Life's most difficult trials are not meant to destroy us but to build resilience and character.

Letting Go

When Joseph finally revealed himself to his brothers, he wept—not just from sorrow, but from release. His tears marked the moment he let go of the past. Forgiveness didn't erase what had happened, but it freed him from being bound to it. The same act of forgiveness that brought Joseph closure also brought reconciliation to his family.

You, too, can make the choice to release past wounds. Decide today that you will not allow yesterday's pain to hinder tomorrow's progress. Embrace the journey, honor your growth, and celebrate the strength you've gained. Life may have tested you, but you are still standing—stronger, wiser, and more prepared for what lies ahead.

* * *

Heavenly Father, help me to release the burdens of the past and walk in the freedom of Your healing. When old wounds resurface, remind me that You are my refuge and my strength. Teach me to forgive, to grow, and to embrace the new things You are doing in my life. I trust that You are working all things together for my good.

In Jesus' Name, Amen.

Chapter 16

Passing the Hurt Test

> You intended to harm me, but God intended it for
> good, to accomplish what is now being done—the
> saving of many lives.
>
> — Genesis 50:20 (NIV)

Working in the prison was not a dead end but the next phase called "prophetic" training by guardians and trustees. In Galatians chapter 4, the Bible says as long as an heir is immature, he is under the subject of trustees and guardians. Although he is the heir, his or her immaturity is going to disqualify them from the promotion of the Father. If we humble ourselves under the mighty hand (plans) of God, He will exalt us. That requires being teachable and flexible.

I am very sorry, but you will not be able to pick your teachers, guardians, and trustees on this one. I know you would like to pick the ones with the nice attitude—the pushovers who will let you manipulate what you want to do without consequences. But often, the ones God chooses will be sharp, gritty like sandpaper, and fiery —all great elements for polishing, sculpting, and purification.

It's not all about the gifts if the heart is not pure before the One with seven eyes—aka perfect vision. When John saw Jesus Christ in heaven as the Lamb with seven eyes and seven horns, that represented perfect insight. Our God sees deeper than what we cover ourselves with; He sees past what we hide behind.

Many wonder, why is it taking so long? Maybe it's God, or maybe it's us. He makes everything beautiful in His own time. Anything that is alive will get off the grill when the fire comes on. It's in those moments that we are tempted to quit the refining process of training. But these are the moments when we must allow God to give us a broken and contrite heart—one that moves only when He says move and does only what He wants us to do.

This is when we consider nothing worthy of holding back from God. If He doesn't want it, we allow Him to burn it up.

Joseph asked one of the men he blessed to remember him. Yet time went by, and Joseph felt forgotten. But if Pharaoh's servant had remembered and released Joseph too soon, Egypt and the Messianic tribes—where Christ was called to come from—would have perished in the famine. The delay was purposeful for the table you will one day sit at.

I know the feeling of seeing God with you in small victories, yet still having a dream in your heart. Many hardworking people come home tired, knowing deep down, "There's something else I would love to do—something I would truly thrive in. But my time is occupied with daily life."

Don't be weary in well-doing. I decree and declare the Lord will crown your year with a path of gold to a door of opportunity set for you.

The truth is, the original can be better than the revised version, and sometimes the revised is better than the original. It's up to God's perfect plan. The New Testament is a greater contract that offers more benefits than the Old Testament. Let the perfect will of God for you, which was predestined before the creation of the universe, be better than any alternative or new opinion.

Joseph's trials were not a sign of abandonment by God, but they tempted him to feel abandoned—a pain that millions have borne. Yet, his trials were a vehicle to the future place he needed to be.

The tests that God allows in our lives often break something in us that needs to be broken—self-reliance, selfish ambition, codependency on others, and comfort in arrested development. He uses these trials to expand our capacity, preparing us for the greater purpose ahead.

Grief is an inevitable part of the human experience, yet it is often misunderstood or avoided. It comes in many forms—the loss of a loved one, the end of a relationship, missed opportunities, or even the death of a dream. While grief can feel overwhelming, it is not meant to leave us broken. Rather, it is a process that God can use to refine, restore, and reposition us for His greater purpose.

* * *

Heavenly Father, help me release the pain I've carried—every wound, every betrayal, every moment I felt overlooked. Help me not to act out of hurt, but to respond with healing. Teach me to see purpose in my pain and to trust Your plan above my own desire for justice. Like Joseph, may I pass the test by choosing forgiveness over revenge and love over pride. Refine my heart, renew my spirit, and use my story for Your glory.

In Jesus' Name, Amen.

Chapter 17

The Revelation

 Humble yourselves, therefore, under God's mighty
hand, that he may lift you up in due time.

— 1 Peter 5:6 (NIV)

When Joseph was finally called out of prison to appear before Pharaoh, there was a key revelation that we might overlook if we move too quickly. Joseph had to be willing to take off his prison garments, wash himself, and present himself in a manner fit for the royal court. He had to abandon the language and mentality of an inmate and embrace his new identity.

The key takeaway here is that we, too, must be willing to shed the trauma of our past like a robe. Our identity is not defined by our pain, diagnosis, or past experiences, but by who God says we are. As sons of God, we are created to reflect His image and likeness. Joseph stripped off his prison clothes and was dressed appropriately to stand before Pharaoh. Likewise, we must prepare ourselves for the calling ahead, ensuring that we are not only gifted but also equipped with wisdom, character, and the ability to lead.

Joseph was no longer just a dreamer—he was now an administrator. Just as God is the ultimate administrator, Joseph was placed in a position that required him to oversee massive quantities of food and develop sustainable structures. Success in our careers, marriages, or businesses requires more than charisma; it demands preparation, wisdom, and diligence. The time of training is not to be rushed but to be embraced as a season of learning and refinement under God-appointed mentors.

One day, Joseph heard the words, "Joseph, Pharaoh summons you." He had no idea what awaited him, just as we don't know who may be preparing to call on us. Many people may have heard of you without knowing you personally, which is why it is crucial to continue refining and utilizing the gifts God has given you, regardless of your current setting.

During our most challenging times, we can become so consumed by circumstances that we forget our value and the mighty works God is doing through us. Elijah, overwhelmed and feeling alone, prayed for God to take his life. Yet, God reminded him of his purpose. Likewise, I pray that you are refreshed and reminded of your worth, even in times of pressing hardship.

When Joseph was called before Pharaoh, he had to be groomed —Egyptians did not favor beards or the lifestyle of shepherds. Similarly, Daniel, a Hebrew prophet, had a thriving career in Babylon, learning its language and customs while remaining devoted to the God of Israel. The lesson? You may find success in an unfamiliar place—an industry outside of your expectations. God does not create us to live in a box, so don't place your future or potential in one either.

Like Joseph shedding his prison garments, we must let go of the residual effects of our past struggles. This includes learning financial management, developing strong relationships, improving communication skills, and embracing professional growth. Just as dross is removed from gold, our hardships should refine us, not define us.

Maybe you feel like your body, finances, or location is a prison. Isaiah 22:22 says, "He who opens doors that no man can shut and shuts doors that no man can open." God, who loves you with an everlasting love, holds the keys to your breakthrough.

When Joseph appeared before Pharaoh, he provided solutions that even the most seasoned advisors could not. He humbly acknowledged, "It is the Lord who gives interpretation to dreams and mysteries." Some people miss their moment because they refuse to heed the mentors and teachers God has placed in their lives. But those who walk in humility are shaped, sharpened, and positioned to bring divine solutions.

When you are called forth, be content and focused so you can execute your assignment well. Don't be discouraged if those you hoped would support you are absent—God is always with you. After being appointed second in command, Joseph did not merely provide an idea; he took ownership and responsibility for overseeing the project.

Many people recognize problems but lack the heart to seek God for solutions. Joseph learned through his trials that serving others would ultimately lead to his own promotion. He did not use his position for revenge against those who wronged him. If he had been released from prison earlier, he may have returned to his family, but he would not have been in position to save countless lives during the seven-year famine.

Many delays are not from the devil but from God, protecting and preparing us for the right moment. Just as wine is stored on a shelf until the perfect occasion, we must trust that our time will come. When Joseph was reunited with his family, he had the opportunity for revenge, but the Holy Spirit convicted him. Seeking vengeance would only hurt the ones he loved in the long run. He learned that the Lord is the ultimate judge and vindicator.

In the end, Joseph's father, Jacob, was escorted to Egypt with the finest transportation available, and Pharaoh recognized Joseph as a father-like figure. This highlights an important principle: as we grow in influence, we may find ourselves in a position to guide and counsel leaders—even those older or more powerful than us. Daniel, for instance, was highly trusted by Babylonian kings because of his wisdom and integrity.

One of the greatest tests of greatness is the ability to submit to authority while serving with excellence. You may not hold a high-ranking title, but if you have the grace to influence decision-makers for God's purposes, that is a noble calling.

Prayer is our greatest power—the means by which we influence the earth from heaven. When your moment comes, be prepared, remain humble, and walk in the fullness of your calling. Your journey is not just about reaching a position but about stewarding it well for God's glory.

May this revelation encourage you to embrace your process, knowing that God's timing is perfect and He is preparing you for something greater than you can imagine.

* * *

Heavenly Father, thank You for using every season to shape me for what's ahead. Help me to shed past pain and step into who You've called me to be. Teach me to serve with humility, lead with wisdom, and trust Your timing completely. Prepare my heart for the moment You call me forward.

In Jesus' Name, Amen.

Chapter 18

Navigating the Stages of Grief – A Biblical Perspective

Blessed are those who mourn, for they will be comforted.

— Matthew 5:4 (NIV)

rief is a deeply personal and transformative journey, unique to each individual. The Bible provides wisdom, encouragement, and guidance to help us navigate through sorrow without becoming trapped in bitterness, anger, or despair. Each stage of grief presents an opportunity for growth, self-reflection, and deeper reliance on God. Let's explore these stages through a biblical lens.

Denial Stage: Confronting the Reality of Loss

Denial often acts as an emotional buffer, shielding us from the immediate weight of loss. While it can serve as a temporary coping mechanism, prolonged denial can prevent deeper healing. God's truth invites us to move beyond avoidance and face reality with faith.

Jesus reassured Martha in John 11:25: "I am the resurrection and the life. The one who believes in me will live, even though they die." While grief is painful, God's promises stand firm. Through prayer and scripture, we find the strength to process our loss, knowing that His love never fails.

Anger Stage: Wrestling with the Pain

Anger is a natural response to grief, but the Bible warns us to "be angry and do not sin; do not let the sun go down on your anger, and give no opportunity to the devil" (Ephesians 4:26-27). If left unchecked, anger can turn into bitterness, poisoning our hearts.

Job's story demonstrates how suffering can bring hidden emotions to the surface. Job questioned God in his grief, yet God responded with wisdom and grace, leading him to restoration. God is not afraid of our emotions—He invites us to bring them to Him in honesty and trust.

Bargaining Stage: Seeking Answers and Control

The bargaining stage reveals our deep longing to rewrite the past. Like Martha, who told Jesus, "Lord, if you had been here, my brother would not have died" (John 11:21), we question what could have been done differently. This can leave us trapped in guilt, regret, or frustration.

However, God's sovereignty is beyond our understanding. Proverbs 3:5-6 reminds us: "Trust in the Lord with all your heart and lean not on your own understanding." Instead of dwelling on what-ifs, we can surrender our questions and trust that He is working all things for our good.

Depression Stage: Finding Light in Darkness

The weight of loss can lead to a deep sense of sadness, isolation, and despair. Even the psalmist cried out, "Why, my soul, are you downcast? Why so disturbed within me?" (Psalm 42:5). But depression is not the end of the story. The verse continues, "Put your hope in God, for I will yet praise Him, my Savior and my God."

In the midst of sorrow, God draws near. "The Lord is close to the brokenhearted and saves those who are crushed in spirit" (Psalm 34:18). Through prayer, community, and His Word, He offers comfort and strength to endure.

Acceptance Stage: Embracing a New Reality

Acceptance is not about forgetting or minimizing the loss but embracing the reality of life after it. It is true that life changes after loss, but the present is still a gift to be cherished. Acceptance requires courage, flexibility, and finding joy and gratitude in the now.

The Apostle Paul shared his secret to contentment: "I have learned the secret of being content in any and every situation, whether well fed or hungry, whether living in plenty or in want" (Philippians 4:12). Acceptance also involves understanding the free will of others, a principle that extends to relationships.

For example, some parents mourn when their children or grandchildren choose different paths. However, God Himself respects free will, saying, "Choose this day whom you will serve... I have set before you life and death... choose life" (Joshua 24:15, Deuteronomy 30:19). Accepting the choices of others can bring peace, as forcing control contradicts God's design for human freedom.

Acceptance also allows us to see God as our ultimate source of restoration and compensation. Consider Job, who lost everything in Job 1 but was blessed with double in Job 42. This shows that God's blessings far outweigh our losses. Romans 8:18 affirms: "I consider that our present sufferings are not worth comparing with the glory that will be revealed in us." Similarly, 2 Corinthians 4:17 says, "For our light and momentary troubles are achieving for us an eternal glory that far outweighs them all."

God's ability to restore is beautifully expressed in Psalm 113:9: "He settles the childless woman in her home as a happy mother of children." This reflects God's heart to compensate us abundantly when we surrender to Him.

Grief is a process that requires patience, reflection, and faith. Each stage invites us to examine our hearts, trust in God's promises, and move toward healing. Remember, God is not only our Restorer but our ultimate Comforter. When we surrender our pain to Him, we make room for His peace, joy, and abundant restoration.

* * *

Heavenly Father, in moments of sorrow, remind me that You are close to the brokenhearted. Help me to trust You through every stage of grief, knowing that You are working all things for my good. Give me the strength to endure, the faith to believe, and the courage to embrace Your healing.

In Jesus' Name, Amen.

Chapter 19

Growing from Pain

We are hard pressed on every side, but not crushed;
perplexed, but not in despair; persecuted, but not
abandoned; struck down, but not destroyed.

— 2 Corinthians 4:8-9 (NIV)

Pain has a way of revealing what is truly inside us. It strips away pretense and forces us to confront the lingering wounds and emotions buried within our hearts. Joseph's journey teaches us that pain is not just an obstacle—it is a test. God does not allow pain in our lives to break us but to refine us, shape us, and prepare us for something greater.

How Joseph's Heart Was Tested Through His Trials

Joseph's life was marked by hardship—betrayed by his own brothers, sold into slavery, falsely accused, and thrown into prison. Each event could have hardened his heart, making him bitter and resentful. Yet, through it all, Joseph remained faithful. He did not allow his suffering to redefine his character or dim his trust in the Lord.

However, his greatest test was not surviving the pit, enduring slavery, or being wrongfully imprisoned. His defining moment came when he stood face to face with the very people who had wronged him.

When famine struck the land, Joseph's brothers unknowingly found themselves before the very man they had once betrayed. In that moment, Joseph held the power to retaliate, to repay their cruelty with vengeance. But instead of using his position for retribution, he chose mercy. His decision was not just about his personal healing—it was about preserving an entire generation.

Unresolved Pain Can Impact Future Generations

Pain, when left unhealed, does not stay contained. It seeps into our actions, our relationships, and even our lineage. Throughout the Bible, we see how generational wounds breed cycles of dysfunction —Cain's jealousy toward Abel, Esau's resentment toward Jacob, and Joseph's own brothers, whose insecurities led them to betrayal.

If Joseph had chosen bitterness, he could have easily justified taking revenge. His pain could have become the foundation for a new cycle of destruction, altering the course of history. But instead, he chose to break the cycle. His choice to forgive did not just impact his own life—it preserved the future of his family and nation.

We, too, face this choice. Will we allow pain to dictate our actions, or will we surrender it to God? Could we be the ones He has called to break the cycle of hurt in our families? Could our healing be the key to someone else's freedom?

The Freedom of Surrender

Pain, when nurtured, transforms into bitterness, resentment, and unforgiveness. It becomes a prison, keeping us bound to the past and hindering our ability to embrace the future. Holding onto pain does not harm those who have wronged us—it only limits us.

Joseph had to decide whether he would define himself by his suffering or by God's promise. He understood a profound truth:

vengeance belongs to the Lord (Romans 12:19). He let go of the need for retribution and embraced the higher calling of restoration. His surrender to God's plan led to the reconciliation of his family and the fulfillment of his purpose.

True freedom is found in surrender. When we release our pain to God, we open ourselves to healing. When we choose to trust Him as our defender, we are no longer held captive by past wounds. Passing the hurt test is not about pretending the pain never happened—it is about refusing to let it control our future. While we may not be able to rewrite the past, we hold the power to determine how we move forward.

It's Not All About Me

Joseph's story reminds us that our pain is not just about us. His struggles were not just about his personal journey—they were about the future of an entire nation. The same is true for us. Could it be that our trials have a greater purpose? Could we be the ones God is calling to shift the direction of generations to come?

If we pass the hurt test, we position ourselves for divine promotion. God is not seeking perfection—He is seeking surrendered hearts. Hearts that have been tested and purified. Hearts that, like Joseph's, are willing to choose love over bitterness, mercy over vengeance, and purpose over pain.

As we reflect on our own experiences, we must ask ourselves:

- What will I choose?
- Will I allow my pain to refine me or define me?
- Will I pass the test and become a vessel of healing, or will I allow bitterness to take root?

The choice is ours. And with God's grace, we can step into the freedom that comes from surrendering it all to Him.

* * *

Henry Isaac Williams

Heavenly Father, I surrender every hurt, every wound, and every moment of betrayal to You. Help me to pass the test of pain, choosing healing over bitterness and mercy over vengeance. Give me the strength to trust You, knowing that You are using even my deepest struggles for a greater purpose. Let my healing be a testimony that leads others to freedom.

In Jesus' Name, Amen.

Chapter 20

The Beauty of Restoration

I will restore to you the years that the swarming locust
has eaten.

—Joel 2:25 (ESV)

Grief has a way of reshaping us, molding us into people we
never expected to become. Loss is painful, and the
wounds of the past can feel unbearable. Yet, in His sovereignty, God uses grief as a refining fire—purging, strengthening, and
preparing us for greater things. Restoration is not simply about
regaining what was lost; it is about stepping into something even
greater.

Joseph's life is a testimony to the beauty of restoration. He
endured betrayal, false accusations, imprisonment, and years of
separation from his family. Yet, through it all, God's hand was upon
him, orchestrating a plan far beyond what Joseph could have imagined. What others meant for harm, God turned into good (Genesis
50:20).

This chapter explores how grief refines our character, deepens
our faith, and ultimately leads to divine restoration.

Refined Through the Fire of Grief

Grief, though deeply painful, is a tool in God's hands. It strips away distractions, humbles us, and refines our hearts like gold in fire. Joseph's suffering was not in vain—every trial prepared him for the weight of the calling on his life.

The Bible describes Joseph's suffering:

 They bruised his feet with shackles; his neck was put in irons, until the time came to fulfill his dreams. The word of the Lord tested and refined him.

— Psalm 105:18

Just as gold must endure extreme heat to be purified, so too must we walk through seasons of grief for our character to be refined. Pain has a way of revealing what is hidden in our hearts—doubt, fear, bitterness, pride. Joseph's time in prison tested him in ways he never anticipated, but in the end, it prepared him to lead with wisdom, integrity, and compassion.

We, too, must trust the process. Our grief is not wasted. God is using it to shape us, to remove what is unnecessary, and to prepare us for the greater plans He has in store.

From Pain to Purpose

Joseph's journey from the prison to the palace was not accomplished through his own strength but through divine enablement. His restoration was not just about reclaiming what had been lost—it was about stepping into the fullness of his God-ordained purpose.

There are moments when our strength fails us, when the weight of loss feels insurmountable. But it is in those moments that God's grace sustains us. The Bible declares:

> To all who mourn... He will give a crown of beauty
> for ashes, the oil of joy instead of mourning, and a
> garment of praise instead of despair.

— Isaiah 61:3

What a powerful promise! God does not leave us in our grief. He meets us in the ashes of our pain and transforms them into something beautiful. The suffering we endure is not meant to break us but to prepare us for a future beyond what we can see.

Joseph was strengthened by God to endure betrayal, unjust suffering, and isolation. But in the end, he was not just restored—he was elevated. Likewise, God's restoration in our lives does not merely return us to where we were; it propels us forward into something greater.

God's Plan for Restoration

Restoration is a process. We often expect it to mean that life will return to what it once was, but God's definition is higher. He restores by taking us forward, not backward.

Consider Joseph:

- He did not return to his father's house as a shepherd boy. He was elevated to second-in-command over Egypt.
- He did not just regain his family. He became the one to save them from famine and lead them into provision.
- He did not hold onto past pain. He embraced healing and allowed God to rewrite his story.

Joseph's transformation was evident in the names he gave his two sons:

- *Manasseh*: "God has made me forget all my troubles and my father's household."

- *Ephraim*: "God has made me fruitful in the land of my suffering."

This is true restoration—when we no longer dwell on our pain but instead recognize how God has used it for His greater purpose.

Restoration does not mean forgetting. It means healing. It means looking at what hurt us and seeing how God worked through it for our good. It means choosing to live again, to hope again, and to believe that the best is yet to come.

Choose Joy and Embrace Hope

One of the greatest acts of faith is choosing joy in the midst of uncertainty. The enemy wants to keep us trapped in grief, bitterness, and regret, but God calls us forward.

Joseph could have remained stuck in the betrayal of his brothers. He could have allowed anger and resentment to consume him. But he chose forgiveness over bitterness, purpose over pain, and faith over fear.

Likewise, we must choose joy even when life has not unfolded the way we expected. We must embrace hope even when the road ahead is unclear.

The Word of God reminds us:

 I consider that our present sufferings are not worth comparing with the glory that will be revealed in us.

— Romans 8:18

Whatever you have lost, God is able to restore abundantly more than you can ask or imagine (Ephesians 3:20). Grief does not have to be the end of your story. Let it be the beginning of something new. Allow God to take the ashes of your pain and turn them into something beautiful. You are still standing. You are still here. And God is not finished with you yet.

This chapter brings your journey full circle—from grief to restoration, from pain to purpose, from sorrow to joy. It is time to embrace all that God has for you. *The best is yet to come.*

* * *

Heavenly Father, thank You for being the God of restoration. When we walk through loss, grief, and seasons of pain, remind us that You are working all things together for good. Help us to trust the process, knowing that You restore not just what was lost but bring us into something greater. May we choose joy, embrace hope, and walk boldly into the future You have prepared for us.

In Jesus' Name, Amen.

Part Three

Prayers for Strength, Faith, & Restoration

As you journey through life, faith, and personal growth, prayer is a powerful tool that connects us to God's wisdom, strength, and love. Throughout this book, we have explored the trials, victories, and transformation that come from aligning ourselves with God's purpose. But transformation is not a one-time event—it is an ongoing process that requires communion with the Lord.

This section is dedicated to *prayers for strength, faith, and restoration* —a collection of declarations rooted in Scripture to encourage you in every season. Whether you are facing uncertainty, grief, or stepping into a new level of purpose, these prayers will serve as a guide to keep your heart anchored in God's promises.

Take a moment to speak these prayers aloud, meditate on them, and let them nourish your spirit. May they remind you that you are deeply loved, divinely protected, and empowered to live as God's dream and the devil's nightmare.

Chapter 21

Prayer of the Love of God

Praise the Lord, O my inner being! Become overwhelmed with gratitude because God is love (1 John 4:8). He created me out of pure love. "I have set my love upon You" (Psalm 91:14). To know You intimately is my greatest purpose. I desire to love You with my entire being and to know that Your love is more vital to me than oxygen itself. Your love gives me courage (Isaiah 41:10), confidence (Hebrews 4:16), and security, driving away all torment of fear (1 John 4:18).

You have lavished Your love on me, pouring it out without ceasing. You adopted and approved me to become Your son or daughter through faith in Christ Jesus (Ephesians 1:5-6). My circumstances are not the confirmation of Your love, for You are eternal and unchanging (Hebrews 13:8). You know my uprising and my sitting down; You are acquainted with all my ways (Psalm 139:2-3). You know every hair on my head (Luke 12:7) and every detail of the masterpiece body-temple You prepared for me. While You knitted my DNA and chromosomes from my father and mother, You declared with accomplishment, "It is very good" (Genesis 1:31).

Your love is my truth that makes me free (John 8:32). I command my intellect and my emotions to take captive every thought and make it obedient to Christ (2 Corinthians 10:5). I deactivate all memories, idol-thoughts, and ideas that go against the true knowledge of God's love. I lift up the gates of my life so that the light of Your truth and love may flood in (Psalm 24:7). You have given me Your approval; You have declared that I am precious and honorable in Your sight (Isaiah 43:4). You have made me righteous and in good standing with God through Christ, sharing His perfect righteousness with me (2 Corinthians 5:21).

Your love for me is never ceasing (Lamentations 3:22). With lovingkindness, You draw me to Yourself (Jeremiah 31:3). Daily, You fill my cup until it overflows (Psalm 23:5). You load me with benefits and crown me with Your lovingkindness (Psalm 103:4). Your gentleness has made me great (Psalm 18:35). You have adorned me with luxuries reserved for those who worship You in spirit and in truth (John 4:23-24).

I am ecstatic to be one of Your elect, Your hand-picked one, the apple of Your eye (Deuteronomy 32:10). Hallelujah! My search for significance is over. You found me (Luke 15:4-7).

In the mighty Name of Jesus, Amen.

Chapter 22

Prayer of Faith

I believe in my God; it is in You that I rely. I keep You as the focus of my life (Hebrews 12:2). You are the Father of every good and perfect gift (James 1:17). You have given me the measure of faith (Romans 12:3). I have the substance to believe that with God, all things are possible (Matthew 19:26).

I live in the reality that what I see in the natural can change at any moment because faith is my evidence that God desires to intervene (Hebrews 11:1). I believe that faith comes by hearing Your Word (Romans 10:17), and my faith will not become shipwrecked (1 Timothy 1:19). I will stand in faith and not be governed by my emotions (2 Corinthians 5:7).

I believe the Lord's report over any diagnosis, verdict, decree, or condition (Isaiah 53:1). I will be rewarded for my faith because faith pleases God (Hebrews 11:6). My faith will cause God to marvel, to be amazed, astonished, and delighted (Matthew 8:10). My faith is not just what I believe; it is expressed through my actions (James 2:17).

I am bold as a lion (Proverbs 28:1). I will do great exploits because my measure of faith will grow from a mustard seed to the size of a mountain (Matthew 17:20). I will go from faith to greater faith (Romans 1:17). My life will be a testimony of the miraculous (Mark 16:17). Through faith in Him, I have access to grace and peace with God (Romans 5:2).

In the mighty Name of Jesus, Amen.

Chapter 23

Prayer of Hope

O Lord my God, how excellent is Your name. You are the Highest, and Your throne is above all. Glory to Your name! I am confident in who You are. You are good, and there is no evil or darkness in You (1 John 1:5). From every viewpoint, You are wonderful (Psalm 92:5). Therefore, my confidence in You, causing me to triumph, is secure as an anchor of hope (Hebrews 6:19). I will hold fast to the profession of my faith (Hebrews 10:23). My hope is in You (Psalm 39:7). I will glory in You as I grow through the challenges of life, knowing that it will polish my character through experiences (Romans 5:3-4).

You have given me a living hope within, and therefore I will not faint or give up (1 Peter 1:3). This hope gives me the strength to press toward the mark of my high calling in Christ Jesus (Philippians 3:14). I am confident, without any doubt, that the work You have begun in my life, You will perfect and bring to completion (Philippians 1:6).

I will not become weary in well-doing, for the set time of favor is coming (Galatians 6:9). The seeds I have sown in tears, I will one day reap with joy and testimony (Psalm 126:5-6). Therefore, I will be steadfast and immovable, knowing that my labor is not in vain (1 Corinthians 15:58). I am a prisoner of hope (Zechariah 9:12); I will not let doubt and fear separate me from my God, who is my refuge and fortress (Psalm 91:2).

I will receive double compensation for shame (Isaiah 61:7). I am mounting up, preparing to soar, because my hope is steadfast in the Lord (Isaiah 40:31). He is renewing my youth like the eagle's (Psalm 103:5). Christ is my hope of glory (Colossians 1:27), and the glory to come will far outweigh my current sufferings (Romans 8:18). My hope has been tested, and though disappointment tempts me to lose heart, I will hope in the Lord, for He is my exceedingly great reward and my shield (Genesis 15:1; Proverbs 30:5).

I will see the goodness of the Lord in the land of the living (Psalm 27:13). My bones will not be dry; my heart will rejoice and sing (Proverbs 17:22). This hope will turn weeping into joy and mourning into dancing (Psalm 30:11). The God I serve lifts the needy from the ashes and seats them with kings (1 Samuel 2:8). My God, in whom I trust, will shine forth like the morning sun, bringing vindication and justice for the oppressed (Psalm 37:6).

Do not rejoice over me, my enemies, for the Lord upholds me with His right hand (Micah 7:8; Isaiah 41:10). The same Spirit that raised Christ from the grave lives in me and will raise me up (Romans 8:11). For He makes all things work together for the good of those who love Him and are called according to His purpose (Romans 8:28). To the only wise God, immortal and invisible, be glory forever. Amen (1 Timothy 1:17).

In the mighty Name of Jesus, Amen.

Chapter 24

Prayer of Protection

You are my hiding place; glory, hallelujah! Your name is a high tower, and the righteous run into it and are safe. "The name of the LORD is a strong tower; the righteous run to it and are safe" (Proverbs 18:10).

Under Your wings, I take shelter until disaster passes. "He will cover you with His feathers, and under His wings, you will find refuge" (Psalm 91:4). In the cleft of the eternal rock, I find comfort. "The LORD is my rock, my fortress, and my deliverer" (Psalm 18:2). Behind You, I live under Your shadow. "Whoever dwells in the shelter of the Most High will rest in the shadow of the Almighty" (Psalm 91:1). You make me invisible to the enemies of my soul. There is a place that the lion and the vulture cannot find. "You will not fear the terror of night, nor the arrow that flies by day" (Psalm 91:5).

O LORD, it is in You that I make my habitation. You are the high, safe place where I dwell. "For You have been my refuge, a strong tower against the foe" (Psalm 61:3). Therefore, all plagues and diseases shall perish, for the law of Christ has set me free from sin and premature death. "For the law of the Spirit of life in Christ Jesus has set you free from the law of sin and death" (Romans 8:2).

I put on the full armor of God, so I am protected from the assaults of the enemy. "Put on the full armor of God, so that you can take your stand against the devil's schemes" (Ephesians 6:11). The arrows that fly will miss and not stick. "No weapon forged against you will prevail" (Isaiah 54:17). I am exempt from the plans of the wicked, and their inventions will not succeed in hindering, frustrating, or stopping God's will in my life. "Many are the plans in a person's heart, but it is the LORD's purpose that prevails" (Proverbs 19:21).

I am protected by angels who excel in strength as I release the voice of the LORD by proclaiming His Word. "For He will command His angels concerning you to guard you in all your ways" (Psalm 91:11). I have angelic escorts that go with me—security, secret service, goodness and mercy, warrior angels, and messenger angels assigned to bless my coming and going. "Surely goodness and mercy will follow me all the days of my life" (Psalm 23:6).

You have given me authority over all the works of the enemy. "I have given you authority to trample on snakes and scorpions and to overcome all the power of the enemy" (Luke 10:19). In the confidence of the all-powerful One, I condemn the words of evil confederacies and predictions. "No weapon formed against you shall prosper" (Isaiah 54:17). I trample over all unseen forces by sea, land, and air.

In the mighty Name of Jesus, Amen.

Chapter 25

Prayer of Provision

God, You are my provider; every good and perfect gift comes from You. "Every good and perfect gift is from above, coming down from the Father of the heavenly lights, who does not change like shifting shadows" (James 1:17). You delight in my prosperity, and I am sufficient in Your sufficiency. "And God is able to bless you abundantly, so that in all things at all times, having all that you need, you will abound in every good work" (2 Corinthians 9:8). You are the source of everything good. "The earth is the Lord's, and everything in it, the world, and all who live in it" (Psalm 24:1).

I will not lack any good thing because I walk upright. "No good thing does He withhold from those who walk uprightly" (Psalm 84:11). You have given me the power to obtain wealth. "But remember the LORD your God, for it is He who gives you the ability to produce wealth" (Deuteronomy 8:18).

I praise You for the multiplication of the little that I have. "Jesus took the five loaves and two fish, and looking up to heaven, He gave thanks and broke the loaves. Then He gave them to the disciples to distribute to the people" (Matthew 14:19). I praise You for ideas, business plans, services, and creativity to produce multiple streams of income. "For the gifts and the calling of God are irrevocable" (Romans 11:29).

The earth is the Lord's, and the fullness thereof. "The earth is the Lord's, and everything in it, the world, and all who live in it." (Psalm 24:1) I praise You for providing water from a rock, showing us that You have provisions that we don't know of. "He split the rocks in the wilderness and gave them water as abundant as the seas"(Psalm 78:15).

We praise You for the mindset to manage provision. The wisdom of Joseph to see what's coming and systematically prepare with a plan to store more than enough for him and his family—and even a nation. "Now therefore, let Pharaoh look for a discerning and wise man and put him in charge of the land of Egypt" (Genesis 41:33). "Joseph stored up huge quantities of grain, like the sand of the sea; it was so much that he stopped keeping records because it was beyond measure" (Genesis 41:49).

Father, teach us how to not be wasteful but beneficial in our management of what You give to us. "The wise man saves for the future, but the foolish man spends whatever he gets" (Proverbs 21:20). We praise You that our souls are prospering in the truth of who we are: a royal priesthood, kings and priests to our God. "But you are a chosen people, a royal priesthood, a holy nation, God's special possession, that you may declare the praises of Him who called you out of darkness into His wonderful light" (1 Peter 2:9). We have more than enough. "The LORD is my shepherd; I lack nothing" (Psalm 23:1).

In the mighty Name of Jesus, Amen.

Chapter 26

Prayer of Courage

Father, in Jesus' name, You are the Eternal Rock from which I was hewn. "The LORD is my rock, my fortress and my deliverer; my God is my rock, in whom I take refuge." (Psalm 18:2) I am a mighty one, and I will bless the Lord with all my might, for He has made me above and not beneath. "The LORD will make you the head, not the tail; if you pay attention to the commands of the LORD your God that I give you this day and carefully follow them, you will always be at the top, never at the bottom" (Deuteronomy 28:13).

I am Your masterpiece, created before the creation of the universe to do good works. "For we are God's masterpiece. He has created us anew in Christ Jesus, so we can do the good things he planned for us long ago" (Ephesians 2:10). I am here to make an impact. I am strong in the Lord and in the power of Your might. "Finally, be strong in the Lord and in his mighty power" (Ephesians 6:10).

You are my glory and the lifter of my head. "But You, O LORD, are a shield around me, my glory, the One who lifts my head high." (Psalm 3:3) I will not cast away my confidence because I will seize the God-ordained opportunities with courage and tenacity. "So do

83

not throw away your confidence; it will be richly rewarded" (Hebrews 10:35).

Philippians 4:13 in the Amplified Bible (AMP) says:
"I can do all things through Him who strengthens and empowers me [to fulfill His purpose], I am self-sufficient in Christ's sufficiency; I am ready for anything and equal to anything through Him who infuses me with inner strength and confident peace" (Philippians 4:13, AMP).

I am determined to finish my course in life with excellence. "I have fought the good fight, I have finished the race, I have kept the faith" (2 Timothy 4:7).

I may not always be the people's choice, but I am Your choice. "But the LORD said to Samuel, 'Do not consider his appearance or his height, for I have rejected him. The LORD does not look at the things people look at. People look at the outward appearance, but the LORD looks at the heart'" (1 Samuel 16:7).

Like a soldier, I will not be moved. I will be like a tree planted, refusing to die before my appointed time. "Those who are planted in the house of the LORD will flourish in the courts of our God" (Psalm 92:13). "The righteous man will flourish like the palm tree, he will grow like a cedar in Lebanon" (Psalm 92:12).

I will evolve into a greater testimony that proves that God is real. "Let your light shine before others, that they may see your good deeds and glorify your Father in heaven." (Matthew 5:16)
By my God, I can leap over walls and run through troops. "For by You I can run against a troop, and by my God I can leap over a wall" (Psalm 18:29).

Through my God, I can confront any challenge. "The LORD is my light and my salvation—whom shall I fear? The LORD is the stronghold of my life—of whom shall I be afraid" (Psalm 27:1)?

My mind is a nesting place for thoughts of Christ and the downloading from the throne room of God. "Set your minds on things above, not on earthly things" (Colossians 3:2). Wherever the soles of my feet go, I take it for the kingdom, power, and glory of God. "I will give you every place where you set your foot, as I promised Moses" (Joshua 1:3). I am more than a conqueror; I am unstoppable through Him who loves me. "No, in all these things we are more than conquerors through Him who loved us" (Romans 8:37).

In the mighty Name of Jesus, Amen.

Acknowledgments

First and foremost, I extend my deepest gratitude to my best friend, my Heavenly Father, and my confidant—the Lord. He has strengthened me, inspired me, and reminded me that I am more than a conqueror. His love is boundless, making me feel as though I am the only one in the world, yet I know He holds that same love for each of us.

I also want to thank God for blessing me with an incredible family—my grandparents, parents, sibling, cousins, and dear friends from all around the world. Your love, support, and encouragement have been a foundation for me, and I am deeply grateful.

To my beautiful wife and my amazing children—this book is a testament to the legacy I hope to leave for you. May you see through these pages that I have strived to raise the bar of greatness. My greatest desire is for you to stand on my shoulders, go further than I have, and embrace the incredible purpose God has for your lives. I love you more than words can ever express.

About the Author

Henry Isaac Williams affectionately know as Isaac, is a minister, mentor, and career coach with over 20 years of experience guiding individuals through spiritual growth, personal transformation, and the discovery of life purpose. Known for his bold yet compassionate voice, Isaac empowers others to rise from brokenness into identity, healing, and their God-intended, gigantic destiny. Whether preaching from the pulpit, teaching in the classroom, or offering one-on-one counsel, his heart beats for restoration and revival—especially among youth, families, and those navigating difficult life transitions.

As the founder and leader of impactful programs such as *B2M* and *More Than Conquerors Worldwide Enterprise*, Isaac has helped countless people see beyond their pain and press into God's promises. His ministry is rooted in authenticity, biblical truth, and the unwavering conviction that we are all called to become God's dream—while living in such a way that we become the devil's worst nightmare.

This debut work is a powerful testimony of survival, surrender, and supernatural strength. It is an invitation to be awakened, equipped, and unleashed.